Cooking with Kids

Cooking with Kids

Matthew Petchinsky

Cooking with Kids: Recipes Under 20 Minutes
By: Matthew Petchinsky

Introduction: The Joy of Cooking with Kids

Cooking with children is more than just preparing meals; it's a journey of creativity, bonding, and learning that creates cherished memories. In today's fast-paced world, spending quality time together can be a challenge, but the kitchen offers a unique space where families can connect meaningfully. This book, *Cooking with Kids: Recipes Under 20 Minutes*, is designed to make that connection effortless, enjoyable, and fulfilling for busy families.

The Benefits of Cooking with Children

Bringing kids into the kitchen offers numerous benefits that go beyond the plate:

- **Fostering Creativity**: Cooking is a wonderful outlet for creativity. From choosing ingredients to decorating finished dishes, children can explore their imaginations and express themselves in exciting and delicious ways.

- **Building Life Skills**: Learning to cook is a vital life skill. By involving children in meal preparation, you're equipping them with the tools to be self-sufficient and confident in the kitchen as they grow older.

- **Encouraging Healthy Eating**: When children take part in preparing meals, they're more likely to try new foods and make healthier choices. Cooking at home introduces them to the value of fresh ingredients and balanced meals, fostering a positive relationship with food.

- **Strengthening Family Bonds**: The kitchen is a space for collaboration and teamwork. Cooking together creates opportunities for communication, laughter, and shared accomplishments, strengthening the bond between parents and children.

The Importance of Quick and Simple Recipes for Busy Families

In today's world, time is often in short supply. Between work, school, extracurricular activities, and household responsibilities, finding the time to prepare meals can feel daunting. That's why this book is built around the principle of simplicity. The recipes in *Cooking with Kids* are designed to be quick—each one can be completed in under 20 minutes—ensuring that even the busiest families can enjoy quality time together in the kitchen without feeling overwhelmed.

Quick recipes also cater to children's short attention spans, keeping them engaged and enthusiastic throughout the cooking process. By focusing on simple, achievable steps, these recipes build confidence in young cooks and ensure that the experience remains fun and stress-free for everyone involved.

How This Book is Designed for Ease, Fun, and Bonding

This book is structured to make cooking with children a breeze, even for those who may feel less confident in the kitchen. Each recipe is tailored with families in mind:

- **Clear, Step-by-Step Instructions**: Every recipe includes straightforward directions, with special notes to indicate steps that children can handle independently or with minimal supervision.
- **Child-Friendly Techniques**: Recipes highlight age-appropriate tasks, such as mixing, measuring, or decorating, so children can take an active role in meal preparation.
- **Ingredients You Already Have**: The recipes use common, easily accessible ingredients to save time and eliminate stress from shopping.

- **Interactive Elements**: Fun tips, trivia, and simple cooking challenges are sprinkled throughout the book to keep children engaged and learning as they cook.

The chapters are organized to guide you through a variety of meal types, from breakfasts to dinners and even snacks and desserts. Each chapter is designed to offer something for everyone, ensuring that mealtime becomes an opportunity to discover new favorites together.

A Kitchen of Connection and Joy

At its heart, *Cooking with Kids* is about more than food. It's about creating moments of joy, laughter, and love that your family will carry with them for years to come. Whether you're whipping up pancakes for a Saturday morning breakfast or assembling creative snack plates after school, this book provides the tools and inspiration to transform your kitchen into a hub of connection and creativity.

So, tie on those aprons, wash those little hands, and get ready to cook up not just meals but also memories. Together, we'll embark on a delicious adventure that nourishes not only the body but also the heart and soul. Let's make cooking with kids a delightful and cherished tradition in your home!

Chapter 1: Getting Started: Setting Up a Kid-Friendly Kitchen

Cooking with kids begins with creating a safe, welcoming, and accessible environment. A well-prepared kitchen not only encourages children to participate but also ensures their safety while fostering independence and confidence. This chapter will guide you through the essentials of setting up a kid-friendly kitchen, from organizing your space to teaching the foundational rules of safety and hygiene.

Organizing Your Kitchen for Kids

An organized kitchen makes cooking with children more efficient, enjoyable, and safe. Here are some tips to create a space that's inviting and practical:

- **Designate a "Kid Zone"**: Allocate a specific area of your kitchen for children's activities. This space could include a sturdy countertop, a small table, or even a step stool to help them reach the counter. Ensure this area is away from hazards like stovetops, sharp objects, or heavy appliances.
- **Use Accessible Storage**: Keep child-friendly tools, utensils, and ingredients within easy reach. Consider using low shelves, clear bins, or labeled containers for items like measuring cups, mixing bowls, and frequently used ingredients (e.g., flour, sugar, or spices).
- **Invest in a Stable Step Stool**: A good-quality, slip-resistant step stool is essential for younger children who need a height boost to work at the counter. Look for one with safety rails for added stability.
- **Create a Safe Workspace**: Ensure the work area is free from clutter and hazards. Use non-slip mats under cutting boards and have child-sized tools available to reduce the risk of accidents.

Essential Tools and Ingredients for Quick Recipes

Having the right tools and pantry staples on hand ensures you're always ready to whip up a quick recipe with your little helpers. Here's a list to get you started:

Kid-Friendly Tools

1. **Child-Safe Knives**: These are designed to cut food but not fingers. Look for ones with rounded tips and grips suitable for small hands.
2. **Measuring Cups and Spoons**: Brightly colored or easy-to-hold sets can make measuring ingredients fun and engaging.
3. **Small Mixing Bowls**: Lightweight, non-breakable bowls are ideal for children to mix ingredients without fear of dropping them.
4. **Silicone Baking Mats**: These are non-stick, easy to clean, and perfect for rolling dough or baking.
5. **Mini Whisks and Spatulas**: Smaller tools are easier for kids to handle and make them feel like real chefs.
6. **Aprons and Towels**: Kid-sized aprons protect clothes, and having extra towels on hand ensures quick cleanup for spills.
7. **Rolling Pins and Cookie Cutters**: Perfect for introducing kids to baking tasks like rolling out dough or cutting fun shapes.
8. **Sturdy Storage Containers**: Use these for pre-measured ingredients to simplify cooking steps for younger children.

Essential Ingredients

- **Dry Goods**: Flour, sugar, oats, rice, pasta, breadcrumbs.
- **Quick Protein Options**: Eggs, shredded cheese, deli meats, canned beans.
- **Fruits and Vegetables**: Fresh or frozen produce that can be quickly chopped or cooked, such as bananas, apples, carrots, and broccoli.
- **Pantry Staples**: Cooking oils, butter, salt, pepper, baking powder, and spices like cinnamon.
- **Ready-to-Go Snacks**: Yogurt, peanut butter, crackers, or granola for easy snack recipes.

Stocking your kitchen with these basics will ensure you're always prepared for impromptu cooking sessions, making it easier to stay on schedule without compromising on fun.

Teaching Kitchen Safety and Hygiene

Safety and hygiene are non-negotiable when cooking with children. Teaching these rules early on ensures that your kitchen remains a safe and enjoyable space for everyone.

Basic Kitchen Safety Tips

1. **Always Supervise**: Never leave children unattended in the kitchen, especially near sharp objects, hot surfaces, or heavy appliances.
2. **Teach the "Hot Zone" Rule**: Explain the dangers of stovetops, ovens, and other hot surfaces. Use colorful tape or mats to mark areas that are off-limits.
3. **Use Age-Appropriate Tools**: Reserve sharp knives, graters, and heavy pots for adults or older children with supervision.
4. **Secure Loose Items**: Keep cords, knives, and small appliances out of reach when not in use.
5. **Handle Spills Immediately**: Clean up spills as soon as they happen to avoid slips and falls.
6. **Demonstrate Proper Techniques**: Show children how to hold utensils correctly, stir gently, and pour carefully to minimize mess and accidents.

Hygiene Rules for Little Cooks

1. **Wash Hands Before Starting**: Teach children to wash their hands thoroughly with soap and water for at least 20 seconds before handling food.
2. **Tie Back Hair**: Long hair should be tied back to prevent it from getting into food or flames.
3. **Wear an Apron**: This keeps clothing clean and minimizes the spread of germs.
4. **Handle Food Safely**: Teach kids to avoid licking fingers, double-dipping utensils, or touching their face while cooking.
5. **Separate Raw Ingredients**: Emphasize the importance of keeping raw meats and eggs away from other foods to avoid cross-contamination.
6. **Clean as You Go**: Encourage children to wipe surfaces and rinse tools as they work, making cleanup easier and teaching responsibility.

Building Confidence in the Kitchen

By organizing your kitchen thoughtfully, equipping it with kid-friendly tools, and teaching safety and hygiene from the start, you're setting the stage for a lifetime of culinary confidence and creativity. Starting with these foundational steps ensures that your kitchen is not only a safe environment but also a place where children feel empowered and excited to contribute.

In the chapters ahead, you'll discover a variety of quick and simple recipes designed to make cooking together an enjoyable and rewarding experience. But first, take a moment to get your kitchen ready. When you're prepared, every recipe becomes an opportunity to share laughter, learning, and love with your little chefs.

Chapter 2: Breakfast Made Easy

Mornings can be one of the busiest times of the day, but they're also a golden opportunity to spend quality time with your children in the kitchen. Breakfast is the most important meal of the day, and when kids are involved in preparing it, they're more likely to eat it with enthusiasm. This chapter offers quick, fun breakfast ideas that your little chefs can help make, as well as tips to turn breakfast prep into an enjoyable, creative bonding activity.

Quick and Fun Breakfast Ideas

Breakfast doesn't have to be complicated to be delicious and nutritious. Here are some simple and engaging ideas that kids will love to prepare and eat:

1. **2-Minute Scrambled Egg Muffins**
   These bite-sized egg muffins are easy to customize with your kids' favorite ingredients and can be made in a microwave for a super-fast breakfast.

Ingredients (makes 4 muffins):

- ◦ 4 large eggs
- ◦ ¼ cup shredded cheese (cheddar, mozzarella, or your choice)
- ◦ ¼ cup diced vegetables (e.g., bell peppers, spinach, tomatoes)
- ◦ 2 tablespoons cooked bacon or ham (optional)
- ◦ Salt and pepper to taste

Steps:

- ◦ Crack the eggs into a large measuring cup and whisk until combined.

- ◦ Add cheese, vegetables, meat (if using), and seasonings. Mix well.
- ◦ Lightly grease a microwave-safe muffin mold or small ramekins.
- ◦ Pour the mixture evenly into the molds.
- ◦ Microwave each muffin for 1–2 minutes or until the eggs are set.
- ◦ Allow to cool slightly before serving.

Kid-Friendly Tasks:

- ◦ Crack the eggs and whisk them.
- ◦ Add and mix in the ingredients.
- ◦ Help grease the molds.

2.Smoothie Bowls

Smoothie bowls are colorful, nutrient-packed, and perfect for letting kids express their creativity by adding fun toppings.

Ingredients (serves 2):

- - 1 cup frozen berries (strawberries, blueberries, or raspberries)
  - 1 banana
  - ½ cup yogurt (Greek or regular)
  - ½ cup milk (dairy or non-dairy)
  - Toppings: granola, sliced fruits, shredded coconut, chia seeds, or nuts

Steps:

- - Blend the frozen berries, banana, yogurt, and milk until smooth.
  - Pour the mixture into bowls.
  - Let your child add their favorite toppings to create a fun design or pattern.

Kid-Friendly Tasks:

- - Measure and pour ingredients into the blender.
  - Select and sprinkle toppings.
  - Use a spoon to create swirls or designs.

3.Overnight Oats

Overnight oats are a no-cook, make-ahead breakfast that's both healthy and customizable.

Ingredients (makes 1 jar):

- - ½ cup rolled oats
  - ½ cup milk (dairy or non-dairy)
  - ¼ cup yogurt
  - 1 teaspoon honey or maple syrup
  - Toppings: fresh fruits, nuts, chocolate chips, or seeds

Steps:

- - In a mason jar or airtight container, combine the oats, milk, yogurt, and sweetener. Stir well.
  - Seal the jar and refrigerate overnight (or for at least 6 hours).
  - In the morning, add your favorite toppings and enjoy!

Kid-Friendly Tasks:

- - Measure and mix ingredients in the jar.
  - Choose and add toppings in the morning.
  - Shake the sealed jar to mix everything.

Tips for Turning Breakfast Prep into a Creative and Engaging Activity

Cooking breakfast together can be much more than just making a meal—it can be a fun and educational experience. Here's how to keep your kids engaged:

1. **Create a Morning Playlist**
   Set the tone with upbeat music that gets everyone in the mood to cook. Let your kids pick some of their favorite songs to make the experience even more enjoyable.

2. **Make It a Game**
   Turn breakfast prep into a playful challenge. For example:
   - Who can whisk the eggs the fastest?
   - Can we arrange toppings to make a smiley face or animal shape?
   - How many colors can we add to our smoothie bowl?

3. **Introduce Learning Moments**
   Use breakfast prep as an opportunity to teach:
   - **Math Skills**: Measuring ingredients and counting toppings.
   - **Colors and Shapes**: Identifying different fruits, vegetables, or tools.
   - **Nutritional Awareness**: Talking about the health benefits of the ingredients being used.

4. **Personalize Recipes**

   Let your kids customize their meals by choosing add-ins for recipes. This autonomy encourages them to take ownership of their creations and builds confidence.

5. **Use Fun Tools and Gadgets**

   Invest in child-friendly utensils, like colorful measuring spoons or animal-shaped cutters. These make the cooking process more enjoyable for little hands.

6. **Celebrate Their Efforts**

   Always praise your child's contributions in the kitchen. Even small tasks, like stirring or sprinkling toppings, deserve recognition to keep them motivated and excited to cook.

The Breakfast Bonding Experience

Breakfast is the perfect time to come together as a family and start the day with positivity. By involving your kids in the kitchen, you're not just creating meals—you're fostering creativity, teaching life skills, and building lasting memories. Whether it's the joy of making egg muffins, designing smoothie bowls, or shaking up jars of overnight oats, these simple activities can turn ordinary mornings into extraordinary moments.

With these quick and fun breakfast ideas, your mornings will never feel rushed or mundane again. Instead, they'll be filled with laughter, learning, and delicious food prepared by the whole family.

Chapter 3: Lunchtime Favorites

Lunchtime is a wonderful opportunity to engage your kids in the kitchen and introduce them to delicious, nutritious meals. This chapter is packed with easy-to-make recipes that are both kid-approved and parent-friendly, tips for creating colorful and balanced plates, and strategies for helping even the pickiest eaters explore new flavors.

Easy-to-Make Lunch Recipes Kids Will Love

Here are three simple, fun, and nutritious lunch ideas that kids can help prepare:

Mini Wraps

Mini wraps are a versatile, hands-on meal that kids can personalize with their favorite fillings. They're perfect for lunch at home or on the go.

Ingredients (makes 4 wraps):

- 4 small flour tortillas
- 4 tablespoons cream cheese, hummus, or avocado spread
- 4 slices deli turkey, ham, or chicken (optional)
- 1 cup shredded lettuce or baby spinach
- ½ cup shredded carrots or sliced cucumbers
- ½ cup shredded cheese (optional)

Steps:

1. Spread cream cheese, hummus, or avocado evenly across each tortilla.
2. Add a slice of deli meat (if using) and layer with lettuce, carrots, and other veggies.
3. Sprinkle cheese on top, if desired.

4. Roll the tortillas tightly into wraps, then slice them into pinwheels or leave them whole.
5. Secure with toothpicks for easy handling.

Kid-Friendly Tasks:

- Spread the cream cheese or hummus.
- Arrange the fillings on the tortillas.
- Help roll the wraps.

Rainbow Pasta Salad

This vibrant, veggie-packed pasta salad is a feast for the eyes and the stomach. Kids love the colors and shapes, and it's a great way to sneak in some extra vegetables.

Ingredients (serves 4):

- 2 cups cooked tri-color rotini or any fun-shaped pasta
- ½ cup cherry tomatoes, halved
- ½ cup diced bell peppers (red, yellow, or orange)
- ½ cup steamed broccoli florets
- ¼ cup shredded carrots
- ½ cup cubed mozzarella or cheddar cheese
- 2 tablespoons Italian dressing

Steps:

1. Combine the cooked pasta and veggies in a large bowl.
2. Add the cheese cubes and drizzle with Italian dressing.
3. Toss everything together until evenly coated.
4. Serve immediately or chill in the fridge for later.

Kid-Friendly Tasks:

- Rinse the veggies.
- Add ingredients to the bowl.
- Toss the salad gently with a spoon or tongs.

Veggie-Packed Quesadillas

These crispy, cheesy quesadillas are loaded with veggies, making them a healthy and satisfying lunch option.

Ingredients (makes 2 quesadillas):

- 4 medium flour tortillas
- 1 cup shredded cheese (cheddar, mozzarella, or a blend)
- ½ cup diced bell peppers
- ½ cup corn kernels (canned or frozen, thawed)
- ½ cup diced tomatoes or salsa
- 1 tablespoon olive oil

Steps:

1. Heat a non-stick skillet over medium heat.
2. Place one tortilla in the skillet and sprinkle half the cheese over it.
3. Add the veggies evenly, then top with the remaining cheese and a second tortilla.
4. Cook for 2–3 minutes on each side until golden and the cheese is melted.
5. Remove from the skillet, slice into wedges, and serve with sour cream or guacamole.

Kid-Friendly Tasks:

- Sprinkle cheese and veggies onto the tortilla.
- Help flip the quesadilla with supervision.
- Arrange the slices on a plate.

Making Lunches Nutritious and Colorful

A colorful plate not only looks appealing but also ensures a variety of nutrients. Here's how to make your kids' lunches vibrant and well-balanced:

- **Include a Rainbow of Vegetables and Fruits**: Bright colors often signify a wide range of vitamins and minerals. Add cherry tomatoes (red), carrots (orange), spinach (green), blueberries (blue), and bell peppers (yellow) to their plates.
- **Balance Protein, Carbs, and Fats**: Combine lean proteins (e.g., turkey, eggs, cheese), whole grains (e.g., tortillas, pasta), and healthy fats (e.g., avocado, olive oil) for a satisfying meal.
- **Use Fun Shapes and Tools**: Cut sandwiches, cheese, or fruits into shapes using cookie cutters to make meals more visually appealing.
- **Serve Dips and Sauces**: Pair veggies with hummus, yogurt-based dips, or guacamole to make them more enticing.

Techniques for Encouraging Picky Eaters to Try New Foods
Dealing with picky eaters can be challenging, but there are effective ways to help children broaden their tastes and embrace new foods:

1. **Make It Fun**: Present foods in playful, creative ways. For example, create a "rainbow plate" challenge where your child tries a food of every color.
2. **Involve Them in the Process**: When kids have a hand in preparing their meals, they're more likely to try what they've made. Let them choose toppings, assemble wraps, or mix salads.
3. **Start Small**: Introduce new foods in tiny portions alongside familiar favorites. For example, add a few spinach leaves to their wrap or a single broccoli floret to their pasta salad.
4. **Pair Familiar with New**: Combine a new ingredient with a food they already love, such as adding diced veggies to cheesy quesadillas.
5. **Be Patient and Persistent**: It can take multiple exposures to a new food before a child is willing to try it. Stay positive and avoid forcing them to eat it.
6. **Lead by Example**: Kids are more likely to eat vegetables if they see adults enjoying them. Make family meals a time to model healthy eating habits.
7. **Reward Exploration**: Celebrate small victories when your child tries a new food. A sticker chart or verbal praise can be effective incentives.

Building a Love for Lunchtime

Lunchtime doesn't have to be a struggle. By involving your kids in the preparation, keeping meals colorful and balanced, and encouraging them to try new foods, you can turn lunch into a time of discovery and connection. Recipes like mini wraps, rainbow pasta salad, and veggie-packed quesadillas are not only quick and easy to make but also serve as building blocks for lifelong healthy eating habits.

In the next chapter, we'll dive into snack time—a magical part of the day where creativity and deliciousness collide. Let's keep the fun and flavor going!

Chapter 4: Dinner in a Flash

Dinnertime is a special moment to come together as a family, share stories about the day, and enjoy a hearty meal. But for many busy families, it can also feel like a race against the clock. This chapter is here to help! With quick, family-friendly dinner recipes that are easy to prepare, you can whip up satisfying meals in no time while involving your kids in the process. Dinner will transform from a chore into a bonding experience that the whole family looks forward to.

Quick and Satisfying Family-Friendly Dinner Recipes

Mini Pizzas on Flatbreads

These mini pizzas are a crowd-pleaser, customizable, and ready in minutes. They're perfect for letting kids express their culinary creativity.

Ingredients (serves 4):

- 4 small flatbreads or naan bread
- 1 cup pizza sauce
- 1½ cups shredded mozzarella cheese
- ½ cup sliced pepperoni, diced ham, or cooked chicken (optional)
- 1 cup assorted toppings: diced bell peppers, sliced olives, mushrooms, pineapple, or spinach
- 1 teaspoon Italian seasoning

Steps:

1. Preheat the oven to 375°F (190°C) or set a toaster oven to bake.
2. Lay the flatbreads on a baking sheet.
3. Spread a thin layer of pizza sauce on each flatbread.
4. Sprinkle shredded cheese evenly over the sauce.
5. Let your kids add their favorite toppings.
6. Sprinkle Italian seasoning on top for extra flavor.
7. Bake for 7–10 minutes, or until the cheese is melted and bubbly.
8. Slice into quarters and serve warm.

Kid-Friendly Tasks:

- Spread the pizza sauce.
- Sprinkle cheese and toppings.
- Arrange the pizzas on the baking sheet.

Stir-Fried Noodles with Veggies

This quick stir-fry is a one-pan wonder packed with flavor and nutrients. It's great for introducing kids to new vegetables in a fun way.

Ingredients (serves 4):

- 8 ounces cooked noodles (spaghetti, ramen, or rice noodles)
- 2 tablespoons vegetable oil
- 1 cup shredded carrots
- 1 cup broccoli florets
- ½ cup sliced bell peppers
- 2 tablespoons soy sauce
- 1 tablespoon honey or maple syrup
- 1 teaspoon minced garlic
- Optional: 1 scrambled egg or cooked chicken/tofu for added protein

Steps:

1. Heat the oil in a large skillet or wok over medium heat.
2. Add the garlic and sauté for 30 seconds until fragrant.
3. Stir in the carrots, broccoli, and bell peppers, and cook for 3–5 minutes until tender-crisp.
4. Add the cooked noodles to the skillet and toss to combine.
5. Mix the soy sauce and honey, then pour over the noodles and veggies. Toss well to coat.
6. Add scrambled egg or protein, if desired.
7. Serve hot, garnished with sesame seeds or green onions if available.

Kid-Friendly Tasks:

- Mix the sauce ingredients in a small bowl.
- Rinse and arrange the vegetables.
- Toss the noodles in the skillet under supervision.

15-Minute Tacos

Tacos are a lifesaver for busy nights! With simple, versatile ingredients, this dinner comes together in no time and is perfect for kids to assemble themselves.

Ingredients (serves 4):

- 8 small taco shells (soft or hard)
- 1 pound ground beef, turkey, or plant-based crumbles
- 1 packet taco seasoning
- ½ cup water
- 1 cup shredded lettuce
- 1 cup diced tomatoes
- ½ cup shredded cheese
- ½ cup sour cream or guacamole
- Optional: salsa, black beans, or corn

Steps:

1. Heat a skillet over medium-high heat and cook the ground meat until browned. Drain any excess fat.
2. Stir in taco seasoning and water, then simmer for 2–3 minutes until well-coated.
3. Warm the taco shells in the oven or microwave.
4. Set up a taco-building station with lettuce, tomatoes, cheese, and toppings in separate bowls.
5. Let everyone assemble their tacos as they like.

Kid-Friendly Tasks:

- Arrange toppings in bowls.

- Fill taco shells with their choice of ingredients.
- Sprinkle cheese and add dollops of sour cream or guacamole.

Suggestions for Making Dinnertime Fun and Efficient

Dinner preparation is the perfect time to bond, teach skills, and let your kids feel like valued contributors to the household. Here's how to make it fun and stress-free:

1. Delegate Tasks Based on Age

- **Younger Kids (Ages 3–6)**: Simple tasks like sprinkling cheese, arranging toppings, or mixing sauces are perfect for little hands.
- **Older Kids (Ages 7–10)**: Encourage them to chop soft vegetables with a child-safe knife or help stir ingredients on the stovetop under supervision.
- **Pre-Teens and Teens**: Allow them to take on more challenging responsibilities, such as browning meat, boiling noodles, or following simple recipes.

2. Make It Interactive

Turn dinner into an activity with these ideas:

- Create a "build-your-own" station for tacos, pizzas, or salads.
- Have kids design their plate with a mix of colors or ingredients.
- Name dishes after family members—e.g., "Sam's Super Stir-Fry" or "Mom's Marvelous Mini Pizzas."

3. Keep Cleanup Simple

Minimize mess by:

- Lining baking sheets with parchment paper for easy disposal.
- Using one-pot or one-pan recipes to reduce dishwashing.
- Teaching kids to clean as they go—wipe counters, rinse tools, and put away ingredients after use.

4. Celebrate Success

Praise your children's efforts in the kitchen, even if things don't turn out perfectly. A sense of accomplishment makes them excited to cook again.

5. Plan Ahead

Prepare ingredients ahead of time for even quicker meals. Pre-chopped veggies, shredded cheese, or cooked proteins can save valuable minutes during busy evenings.

The Power of Shared Dinners

Dinner isn't just about nourishing the body; it's also a time to strengthen family connections. By involving your kids in the preparation, you're creating a routine that prioritizes teamwork, creativity, and communication. Recipes like mini pizzas, stir-fried noodles, and tacos are simple enough for busy nights yet packed with opportunities for fun and collaboration.

With these tips and recipes, dinnertime can go from stressful to stress-free in a flash. Ready to tackle dessert next? Stay tuned for the sweet and exciting ideas in the following chapter!

Chapter 5: Sweet Treats and Snacks

Snack time and dessert don't have to mean sugary indulgence. Instead, they can be opportunities to teach kids about balancing sweetness with nutrition while satisfying their cravings. This chapter focuses on quick and fun-to-make recipes like fruit kabobs, no-bake energy bites, and yogurt parfaits. These recipes are kid-friendly, require minimal preparation, and strike the perfect balance between deliciousness and health.

Quick Desserts and Snack Recipes Kids Can Help Create
Fruit Kabobs

Fruit kabobs are colorful, customizable, and packed with natural sweetness. They're perfect for a quick snack or a fun dessert that doubles as a hands-on activity for kids.

Ingredients (makes 8 kabobs):

- 1 cup strawberries, hulled
- 1 cup pineapple chunks
- 1 cup seedless grapes (red or green)
- 1 banana, sliced into rounds
- Optional: mini marshmallows or small cubes of cheese

Steps:

1. Wash and dry the fruits thoroughly.
2. Provide kids with bamboo skewers (with blunted tips for safety) or sturdy plastic straws.
3. Let them thread the fruits onto the skewers in any pattern they like.
4. Optional: Serve with a side of yogurt or a drizzle of honey for dipping.

Kid-Friendly Tasks:

- Wash the fruits.
- Thread fruits onto the skewers.
- Arrange the kabobs on a serving plate.

No-Bake Energy Bites

These bite-sized snacks are packed with wholesome ingredients and are perfect for an afternoon pick-me-up. Plus, they're incredibly fun to roll and mix!

Ingredients (makes about 12 bites):

- 1 cup rolled oats
- ½ cup peanut butter or almond butter
- ⅓ cup honey or maple syrup
- ¼ cup mini chocolate chips or raisins
- ¼ cup ground flaxseed or chia seeds
- 1 teaspoon vanilla extract

Steps:

1. In a large bowl, combine all the ingredients and mix until well blended.
2. Cover the mixture and refrigerate for 20–30 minutes to firm up.
3. Once chilled, roll the mixture into small balls using your hands.
4. Store in an airtight container in the fridge for up to a week.

Kid-Friendly Tasks:

- Measure and mix the ingredients.
- Roll the mixture into balls.
- Place the bites into a container.

Yogurt Parfaits

Layered yogurt parfaits are not only visually appealing but also packed with nutrition. Kids can create their own combinations, making snack time a fun and creative experience.

Ingredients (serves 4):

- 2 cups yogurt (Greek or regular, plain or flavored)
- 1 cup granola or crushed cereal
- 1 cup fresh fruits (e.g., blueberries, sliced strawberries, diced mango)
- Optional: a drizzle of honey or a sprinkle of nuts

Steps:

1. Set out all the ingredients in separate bowls.
2. Provide clear cups or glasses for layering.
3. Show kids how to layer yogurt, granola, and fruits, then repeat until the glass is full.
4. Top with a drizzle of honey or sprinkle of nuts, if desired.

Kid-Friendly Tasks:

- Spoon yogurt into the cups.
- Layer granola and fruits.
- Drizzle honey or add nuts for the finishing touch.

Balancing Sweetness with Healthier Ingredients

Desserts and snacks don't need to rely solely on sugar to be satisfying. Here's how to create treats that balance indulgence with nutrition:

- **Use Natural Sweeteners**: Ingredients like honey, maple syrup, and ripe fruits add sweetness without refined sugar.
- **Add Whole Foods**: Incorporate oats, nuts, seeds, and whole grains for added fiber and nutrients.
- **Sneak in Veggies**: For example, add shredded carrots or zucchini to muffins or brownies for a nutrient boost.
- **Choose Better Fats**: Use nut butters or avocados instead of processed fats.

Balancing sweetness with healthier options teaches kids that treats can be both delicious and good for them.

Tips for Teaching Portion Control and Smart Choices

Snack time is a fantastic opportunity to instill lifelong habits like portion control and making thoughtful food choices. Here are some strategies:

1. Emphasize Balance

Teach kids that snacks and desserts are part of a balanced diet and not a replacement for meals. Encourage them to pair treats with a source of protein or healthy fat, like fruit kabobs with cheese or yogurt parfaits with nuts.

2. Use Kid-Sized Portions

Help children recognize appropriate serving sizes by using small plates, bowls, or cups. Show them how much of each snack is enough to satisfy without overindulging.

3. Create a Snack Schedule

Establishing regular snack times helps prevent mindless grazing. Offer snacks between meals, not too close to dinnertime.

4. Involve Them in Choices

Let kids pick their snacks from a pre-approved list of healthy options. This autonomy empowers them to make smart choices and feel in control.

5. Lead by Example

Model healthy snacking habits by enjoying balanced treats yourself. Kids are more likely to follow suit when they see you practicing what you preach.

6. Encourage Mindful Eating

Teach kids to eat slowly and savor their food. This practice helps them recognize when they're full and prevents overeating.

7. Make Treats Special

Position treats as occasional indulgences rather than daily occurrences. This mindset helps children develop a healthy relationship with sweet foods.

Sweet Moments in the Kitchen

Snack time and dessert preparation are perfect opportunities for bonding, teaching, and laughter. Recipes like fruit kabobs, no-bake energy bites, and yogurt parfaits not only satisfy sweet cravings but also teach children valuable skills like portion control, food creativity, and mindful eating.

By making these treats together, you're creating delicious memories while setting the foundation for a lifetime of healthy habits. With every recipe, snack time transforms into a moment of joy and learning that nourishes the body and the heart.

In the next chapter, we'll explore how to make the most of seasonal and holiday treats, adding a festive touch to your family's cooking adventures!

Appendix A: Cooking with Kids Tips and Tricks

Cooking with kids is an exciting and rewarding activity that not only strengthens family bonds but also teaches valuable life skills. However, it's important to tailor the experience to their age and ability, ensuring it's both safe and enjoyable. This appendix provides a detailed guide to age-appropriate tasks and ways to turn your time in the kitchen into a fun learning opportunity.

Age-Appropriate Tasks for Kids

Giving kids tasks suited to their age helps build confidence and keeps them engaged while ensuring safety. Below is a breakdown of activities for different age groups:

Ages 2–3 (The Littlest Helpers)

Toddlers love being involved in simple, safe, and hands-on tasks. Their fine motor skills are still developing, so focus on activities that don't require precision.

Tasks:

- Washing fruits and vegetables.
- Tearing lettuce leaves or herbs.
- Stirring ingredients in a large bowl.
- Sprinkling toppings (cheese, chocolate chips, or nuts).
- Pouring pre-measured ingredients into a mixing bowl.
- Using cookie cutters to make fun shapes.

Tips:

- Keep tasks short and sweet to match their attention span.
- Use non-breakable bowls and utensils.

- Supervise closely to prevent spills or accidents.

Ages 4–6 (The Enthusiastic Assistants)

Preschoolers and early elementary-age kids are eager to help and capable of handling slightly more complex tasks. This is a great time to introduce basic kitchen safety.

Tasks:

- Cracking eggs into a bowl.
- Measuring and leveling dry ingredients.
- Using a hand mixer or whisk.
- Rolling dough or forming shapes (e.g., cookies or meatballs).
- Arranging toppings on pizzas or salads.
- Spreading butter or sauces with a blunt knife.

Tips:

- Teach proper hand-washing before and after handling food.
- Provide child-safe knives for cutting soft items like bananas or cheese.
- Encourage them to clean up small messes to build responsibility.

Ages 7–9 (The Junior Chefs)

At this stage, kids can follow simple instructions, use some kitchen tools, and take pride in completing tasks independently.

Tasks:

- Cutting soft fruits and vegetables with a child-safe knife.
- Grating cheese or zesting citrus (with supervision).
- Mixing batters and doughs.
- Using the stovetop to stir or sauté under supervision.
- Plating and garnishing dishes.

- Operating small appliances like a blender or toaster (with guidance).

Tips:

- Teach basic knife skills, such as how to hold a knife and cut safely.
- Start introducing food safety concepts, like avoiding cross-contamination.
- Let them practice reading simple recipes to develop independence.

Ages 10–12 (The Confident Cooks)

Pre-teens are ready to take on more challenging tasks and can often prepare simple meals with minimal help.

Tasks:

- Using sharp knives with proper technique.
- Cooking on the stovetop and using the oven (with supervision).
- Kneading and rolling out dough.
- Seasoning and tasting food to adjust flavors.
- Following multi-step recipes.
- Cleaning up the kitchen after cooking.

Tips:

- Teach the importance of using oven mitts and being cautious with hot surfaces.
- Encourage creativity in meal preparation, like inventing their own recipes.
- Reinforce the importance of cleaning as they go.

Ages 13+ (The Independent Chefs)

Teenagers can tackle most kitchen tasks independently, making them valuable partners in meal prep.

Tasks:

- Planning and preparing entire meals.
- Baking bread or pastries from scratch.
- Experimenting with advanced techniques, such as caramelizing or grilling.
- Managing time and multitasking in the kitchen.
- Learning to grocery shop and budget for ingredients.

Tips:

- Encourage them to explore cooking as a creative outlet or future career option.
- Introduce cultural cuisines to expand their culinary horizons.
- Emphasize the importance of cleaning and organizing after cooking.

Turning Cooking into a Learning Opportunity

Cooking offers a wealth of educational opportunities that go far beyond food preparation. Here's how to integrate learning into your time in the kitchen:

Math Skills

- **Measuring Ingredients**: Teach fractions by using measuring cups and spoons (e.g., ½ cup + ¼ cup = ¾ cup).
- **Counting and Sequencing**: Count eggs, steps, or layers in a recipe.
- **Basic Arithmetic**: Double or halve a recipe to practice multiplication and division.
- **Time Management**: Use timers and clocks to track cooking times.

Science Concepts

- **Chemical Reactions**: Explain how baking soda and vinegar interact or how heat causes dough to rise.
- **States of Matter**: Discuss the transformation of ingredients (e.g., liquids to solids when making ice cream or batter to cake).
- **Temperature and Heat**: Teach about boiling, steaming, and sautéing and how heat changes food textures.
- **Food Preservation**: Introduce concepts like freezing, refrigeration, and canning.

Language and Literacy

- **Reading Recipes**: Encourage kids to read recipes aloud to practice literacy.
- **Vocabulary Building**: Introduce culinary terms like "simmer," "fold," or "marinate."

- **Storytelling**: Share the history or cultural significance of a dish while cooking.

Art and Creativity

- **Food Presentation**: Let kids design how their dish will look on the plate.
- **Color Mixing**: Experiment with food coloring or garnishes to create visually appealing meals.
- **Creative Combinations**: Encourage them to invent their own recipes or flavor pairings.

Life Skills

- **Teamwork**: Assign roles and work together to complete a recipe.
- **Responsibility**: Emphasize cleaning up and putting away tools after use.
- **Problem-Solving**: Discuss what to do if something goes wrong, like a recipe not turning out as expected.

Final Thoughts on Cooking with Kids

Cooking with kids is an adventure that builds skills, strengthens relationships, and creates lifelong memories. By tailoring tasks to their age and abilities and using the kitchen as a classroom, you're fostering creativity, confidence, and independence. With these tips and tricks, every cooking session can be safe, fun, and full of valuable lessons for kids of all ages.

Appendix B: Ingredient Substitutions and Allergy-Friendly Options

Cooking for a family often means accommodating a variety of dietary needs and preferences. Whether you're dealing with allergies, intolerances, or lifestyle choices, this appendix provides a comprehensive guide to ingredient substitutions that ensure everyone can enjoy the recipes in this book. With these simple swaps, you can create gluten-free, dairy-free, nut-free, or other allergy-friendly dishes without compromising on taste or texture.

General Tips for Ingredient Substitutions

- **Start Small**: When using a substitute for the first time, try it in a small batch to gauge how it affects the recipe.
- **Stick to Similar Functions**: Substitute ingredients with similar properties (e.g., liquid for liquid, fat for fat) to maintain the recipe's consistency and flavor.
- **Check Labels**: Always check labels for hidden allergens or cross-contamination warnings, especially when cooking for someone with severe allergies.

Gluten-Free Substitutions

For those with gluten intolerance or celiac disease, replacing gluten-containing ingredients can be simple with the right substitutes.

Flours

- Replace all-purpose flour with a gluten-free flour blend in a 1:1 ratio for most recipes.
- Alternatives for specific uses:
  - **Baking**: Almond flour, coconut flour (use less as it absorbs more liquid), or oat flour.
  - **Thickening**: Arrowroot powder, cornstarch, or tapioca starch.

Breads and Wraps

- Use gluten-free tortillas, naan, or flatbreads for recipes like mini pizzas or wraps.
- For breadcrumbs, swap with crushed gluten-free crackers, gluten-free panko, or ground nuts.

Pasta

- Substitute regular pasta with gluten-free versions made from rice, quinoa, or chickpeas. Tri-color gluten-free pasta works perfectly for recipes like Rainbow Pasta Salad.

Soy Sauce

- Traditional soy sauce contains wheat. Use tamari or coconut aminos as a gluten-free alternative.

Dairy-Free Substitutions

Avoiding dairy doesn't mean sacrificing flavor. These swaps ensure creamy and delicious results:

Milk

- Replace cow's milk with unsweetened almond milk, oat milk, soy milk, or coconut milk. Choose fortified options for added calcium.

Cheese

- Use dairy-free cheese alternatives made from nuts (e.g., cashew cheese) or plant-based ingredients. Nutritional yeast can also provide a cheesy flavor in savory dishes.

Yogurt

- Opt for dairy-free yogurts made from coconut, almond, or soy milk for recipes like Yogurt Parfaits.

Butter

- Use plant-based margarine, coconut oil, or olive oil in place of butter. For baking, vegan butter sticks are an excellent choice.

Cream

- Substitute heavy cream with coconut cream or cashew cream. For whipping, try aquafaba (the liquid from canned chickpeas) as a light and airy alternative.

Nut-Free Substitutions

Nut allergies can be severe, so it's essential to avoid all forms of nuts, including oils and butters derived from them.

Nut Butters

- Replace peanut or almond butter with sunflower seed butter, soy butter, or tahini.

Flours

- Swap almond flour with oat flour, coconut flour, or a nut-free gluten-free flour blend.

Milks

- Use rice milk, oat milk, or hemp milk as nut-free alternatives to almond or cashew milk.

Cheese Alternatives

- Ensure plant-based cheeses are nut-free; some are made from coconut or starch-based ingredients instead of cashews.

Egg-Free Substitutions

Egg allergies or vegan diets can easily be accommodated with these replacements:

For Binding (1 Egg Equivalent)

- 1 tablespoon ground flaxseed or chia seeds mixed with 3 tablespoons water (let sit for 5 minutes).
- ¼ cup unsweetened applesauce or mashed banana.
- ¼ cup plain yogurt (dairy or non-dairy).

For Leavening (1 Egg Equivalent)

- 2 tablespoons water + 1 tablespoon oil + 1 teaspoon baking powder.
- Commercial egg replacers like Bob's Red Mill Egg Replacer or Ener-G Egg Replacer.

Sugar-Free Substitutions

For those reducing sugar intake or with diabetes, these swaps work well:

Sweeteners

- Replace white sugar with natural options like honey, maple syrup, or agave nectar.
- Use zero-calorie sweeteners like stevia or monk fruit for sugar-free desserts.

Chocolate Chips

- Choose sugar-free or dark chocolate chips made with stevia or erythritol.

Soy-Free Substitutions

For those avoiding soy due to allergies or dietary preferences:

Soy Sauce

- Use coconut aminos as a soy-free alternative.

Soy Milk

- Swap with almond milk, oat milk, or rice milk.

Tofu

- Replace tofu with chickpeas, lentils, or jackfruit in recipes requiring plant-based protein.

Recipe Adaptation Examples
Gluten-Free Mini Pizzas on Flatbreads

- Use gluten-free flatbreads or cauliflower crusts.
- Ensure the pizza sauce and toppings are certified gluten-free.

Dairy-Free Yogurt Parfaits

- Layer dairy-free yogurt with granola and fresh fruit.
- Check that the granola is free from butter or dairy-based ingredients.

Nut-Free Energy Bites

- Replace peanut butter with sunflower seed butter.
- Use chocolate chips labeled as nut-free.

Final Thoughts on Substitutions

Adapting recipes for dietary restrictions doesn't mean compromising on flavor, creativity, or nutrition. With a little planning and the right substitutes, you can ensure that every dish in this book is accessible and enjoyable for everyone in your family. Use this guide as a handy reference to navigate allergies and preferences, making your kitchen a welcoming space for all.

<u>Message from the Author:</u>

I hope you enjoyed this book, I love astrology and knew there was not a book such as this out on the shelf. I love metaphysical items as well. Please check out my other books:

-Life of Government Benefits

-My life of Hell

-My life with Hydrocephalus

-Red Sky

-World Domination:Woman's rule

-World Domination:Woman's Rule 2: The War

-Life and Banishment of Apophis: book 1

-The Kidney Friendly Diet

-The Ultimate Hemp Cookbook

-Creating a Dispensary(legally)

-Cleanliness throughout life: the importance of showering from childhood to adulthood.

-Strong Roots: The Risks of Overcoddling children

-Hemp Horoscopes: Cosmic Insights and Earthly Healing

- Celestial Hemp Navigating the Zodiac: Through the Green Cosmos

-Astrological Hemp: Aligning The Stars with Earth's Ancient Herb

-The Astrological Guide to Hemp: Stars, Signs, and Sacred Leaves

-Green Growth: Innovative Marketing Strategies for your Hemp Products and Dispensary

-Cosmic Cannabis

-Astrological Munchies

-Henry The Hemp

-Zodiacal Roots: The Astrological Soul Of Hemp

- **Green Constellations: Intersection of Hemp and Zodiac**

-Hemp in The Houses: An astrological Adventure Through The Cannabis Galaxy

-Galactic Ganja Guide

Heavenly Hemp

Zodiac Leaves

Doctor Who Astrology

Cannastrology

Stellar Satvias and Cosmic Indicas

Celestial Cannabis: A Zodiac Journey

AstroHerbology: The Sky and The Soil: Volume 1

AstroHerbology:Celestial Cannabis:Volume 2

Cosmic Cannabis Cultivation

The Starry Guide to Herbal Harmony: Volume 1

The Starry Guide to Herbal Harmony: Cannabis Universe: Volume 2

Yugioh Astrology: Astrological Guide to Deck, Duels and more

Nightmare Mansion: Echoes of The Abyss

Nightmare Mansion 2: Legacy of Shadows

Nightmare Mansion 3: Shadows of the Forgotten

Nightmare Mansion 4: Echoes of the Damned

The Life and Banishment of Apophis: Book 2

Nightmare Mansion: Halls of Despair

Healing with Herb: Cannabis and Hydrocephalus

Planetary Pot: Aligning with Astrological Herbs: Volume 1

Fast Track to Freedom: 30 Days to Financial Independence Using AI, Assets, and Agile Hustles

Cosmic Hemp Pathways

How to Become Financially Free in 30 Days: 10,000 Paths to Prosperity

Zodiacal Herbage: Astrological Insights: Volume 1

Nightmare Mansion: Whispers in the Walls

The Daleks Invade Atlantis

Henry the hemp and Hydrocephalus

10X The Kidney Friendly Diet

Cannabis Universe: Adult coloring book

Hemp Astrology: The Healing Power of the Stars

Zodiacal Herbage: Astrological Insights: Cannabis Universe: Volume 2

<u>Planetary Pot: Aligning with Astrological Herbs: Cannabis Universes: Volume 2</u>

Doctor Who Meets the Replicators and SG-1: The Ultimate Battle for Survival

Nightmare Mansion: Curse of the Blood Moon

<u>The Celestial Stoner: A Guide to the Zodiac</u>

Cosmic Pleasures: Sex Toy Astrology for Every Sign

Hydrocephalus Astrology: Navigating the Stars and Healing Waters

Lapis and the Mischievous Chocolate Bar

Celestial Positions: Sexual Astrology for Every Sign

Apophis's Shadow Work Journal: : A Journey of Self-Discovery and Healing

Kinky Cosmos: Sexual Kink Astrology for Every Sign

Digital Cosmos: The Astrological Digimon Compendium

Stellar Seeds: The Cosmic Guide to Growing with Astrology

Apophis's Daily Gratitude Journal

Cat Astrology: Feline Mysteries of the Cosmos

The Cosmic Kama Sutra: An Astrological Guide to Sexual Positions

Unleash Your Potential: A Guided Journal Powered by AI Insights

Whispers of the Enchanted Grove

Cosmic Pleasures: An Astrological Guide to Sexual Kinks

369, 12 Manifestation Journal

Whisper of the nocturne journal(blank journal for writing or drawing)

The Boogey Book

Locked In Reflection: A Chastity Journey Through Locktober

Generating Wealth Quickly:

How to Generate $100,000 in 24 Hours

Star Magic: Harness the Power of the Universe

The Flatulence Chronicles: A Fart Journal for Self-Discovery

The Doctor and The Death Moth

Seize the Day: A Personal Seizure Tracking Journal

The Ultimate Boogeyman Safari: A Journey into the Boogie World and Beyond

Whispers of Samhain: 1,000 Spells of Love, Luck, and Lunar Magic: Samhain Spell Book

Apophis's guides:

Witch's Spellbook Crafting Guide for Halloween

<u>Frost & Flame: The Enchanted Yule Grimoire of 1000 Winter Spells</u>

<u>The Ultimate Boogey Goo Guide & Spooky Activities for Halloween Fun</u>

Harmony of the Scales: A Libra's Spellcraft for Balance and Beauty

The Enchanted Advent: 36 Days of Christmas Wonders

Nightmare Mansion: The Labyrinth of Screams

Harvest of Enchantment: 1,000 Spells of Gratitude, Love, and Fortune for Thanksgiving

The Boogey Chronicles: A Journal of Nightly Encounters and Shadowy Secrets

The 12 Days of Financial Freedom: A Step-by-Step Christmas Countdown to Transform Your Finances

Sigil of the Eternal Spiral Blank Journal

A Christmas Feast: Timeless Recipes for Every Meal

Holiday Stress-Free Solutions: A Survival Guide to Thriving During the Festive Season

Yu-Gi-Oh! Holiday Gifting Mastery: The Ultimate Guide for Fans and Newcomers Alike

Holiday Harmony: A Hydrocephalus Survival Guide for the Festive Season

Celestial Craft: The Witch's Almanac for 2025 – A Cosmic Guide to Manifestations, Moons, and Mystical Events

Doctor Who: The Toymaker's Winter Wonderland

Tulsa King Unveiled: A Thrilling Guide to Stallone's Mafia Masterpiece

Pendulum Craft: A Complete Guide to Crafting and Using Personalized Divination Tools

Nightmare Mansion: Santa's Eternal Eve

Starlight Noel: A Cosmic Journey through Christmas Mysteries

The Dark Architect: Unlocking the Blueprint of Existence

Surviving the Embrace: The Ultimate Guide to Encounters with The Hugging Molly

The Enchanted Codex: Secrets of the Craft for Witches, Wiccans, and Pagans

Harvest of Gratitude: A Complete Thanksgiving Guide

Yuletide Essentials: A Complete Guide to an Authentic and Magical Christmas

Celestial Smokes: A Cosmic Guide to Cigars and Astrology

Living in Balance: A Comprehensive Survival Guide to Thriving with Diabetes Insipidus

Cosmic Symbiosis: The Venom Zodiac Chronicles

The Cursed Paw of Ambition

Cosmic Symbiosis: The Astrological Venom Journal

Celestial Wonders Unfold: A Stargazer's Guide to the Cosmos (2024-2029)

The Ultimate Black Friday Prepper's Guide: Mastering Shopping Strategies and Savings

Cosmic Sales: The Astrological Guide to Black Friday Shopping
Legends of the Corn Mother and Other Harvest Myths
Whispers of the Harvest: The Corn Mother's Journal
The Evergreen Spellbook
The Doctor Meets the Boogeyman
The White Witch of Rose Hall's SpellBook
The Gingerbread Golem's Shadow: A Study in Sweet Darkness
The Gingerbread Golem Codex: An Academic Exploration of Sweet Myths
The Gingerbread Golem Grimoire: Sweet Magicks and Spells for the Festive Witch
The Curse of the Gingerbread Golem
10-minute Christmas Crafts for kids
<u>Christmas Crisis Solutions: The Ultimate Last-Minute Survival Guide</u>
Gingerbread Golem Recipes: Holiday Treats with a Magical Twist
The Infinite Key: Unlocking Mystical Secrets of the Ages
Enchanted Yule: A Wiccan and Pagan Guide to a Magical and Memorable Season
Dinosaurs of Power: Unlocking Ancient Magick
Astro-Dinos: The Cosmic Guide to Prehistoric Wisdom
Gallifrey's Yule Logs: A Festive Doctor Who Cookbook
The Dino Grimoire: Secrets of Prehistoric Magick
The Gift They Never Knew They Needed
The Gingerbread Golem's Culinary Alchemy: Enchanting Recipes for a Sweetly Dark Feast
A Time Lord Christmas: Holiday Adventures with the Doctor
Krampusproofing Your Home: Defensive Strategies for Yule
Silent Frights: A Collection of Christmas Creepypastas to Chill Your Bones
Santa Raptor's Jolly Carnage: A Dino-Claus Christmas Tale
Prehistoric Palettes: A Dino Wicca Coloring Journey
The Christmas Wishkeeper Chronicles

The Starlight Sleigh: A Holiday Journey
Elf Secrets: The True Magic of the North Pole
Candy Cane Conjurations
If you want solar for your home go here: https://www.harborso-
lar.live/apophisenterprises/

Get Some Tarot cards: https://www.makeplayingcards.com/sell/ apophis-occult-shop

Get some shirts: https://www.bonfire.com/store/apophis-shirt-emporium/

<u>**Instagrams:**</u>
@apophis_enterprises,
@apophisbookemporium,
@apophisscardshop
Twitter: @apophisenterpr1
 Tiktok:@apophisenterprise
Youtube: @sg1fan23477, @FiresideRetreatKingdom
Hive: @sg1fan23477
CheeLee: @SG1fan23477

Podcast: Apophis Chat Zone: https://open.spotify.com/show/
5zXbrCLEV2xzCp8ybrfHsk?si=fb4d4fdbdce44dec

Newsletter: https://apophiss-newsletter-27c897.beehiiv.com/

If you want to support me or see posts of other projects that I have come over to: **<u>buymeacoffee.com/mpetchinskg</u>**
I post there daily several times a day

Get your Dinowicca or Christmas themed digital products, especially Santa Raptor songs and other musics. Here: **https://sg1fan23477.gumroad.com**

Apophis Yuletide Digital has not only digital Christmas items, but it will have all things with Dinowicca as well as other Digital products.

* 9 7 9 8 3 3 0 6 9 4 6 7 9 *